OREGON POETRY ASSOCIATION

CASCADIA

The Student Poetry Contest
Anthology of Prize-Winning Poems

The Student Poetry Contest exists to meet a need
that is often overlooked in today's fast-paced society:
a child's imagination needs exercise, too.

Spring 2013   **Number 15**

Oregon Poetry Association
P.O. Box 14582
Portland, Oregon 97293

www.oregonpoets.org

PRINTED IN THE UNITED STATES OF AMERICA

OPA is recognized for artistic achievement by
the Oregon Arts Commission, which is supported in part by
the National Endowment for the Arts.

Published by:
Arrowcloud Press
Editor:
C.S. Blue

Proofreaders:
Tiel Aisha Ansari
Quinton Hallett
Nancy Carol Moody

Cover photo and inside photos by:
Judy Hayden
Eugene, Oregon

OREGON STUDENT POETS SHINE AGAIN IN COMPETITION—

Oregon Poetry Association Student Poetry Contest 2013
Contest Chair's Statement

In a year of educational budget cuts across the state—a year when teachers saw valued colleagues let go, and when three people stretched to cover the work of five—in a year of heartbreak and struggle and crisis for many schools, teachers across Oregon found the time to help their students write and submit poems for OPA's fifteenth annual student contest.

You now hold some of these poems in your hands.

These forty poems were selected from over six hundred entries. Judges included Mark Alter, former OPA president David Hedges, Tom Lavoie, Anatoly Molotkov, Duane Poncy, Ryan Scariano, Kelly Sievers, Friends of William Stafford board member Leah Stenson, Emily Sterling, and Armin Tolentino. All gathered at Portland's Marshall High School campus to read stacks of poems and rank them for judging.

Poems were judged by age category: kindergarten through second grade, third through fifth grade, sixth through eighth grade, and high school. In each category, three winners and seven honorable mentions were selected. All winning and honorable mention poems in the middle and high school categories were forwarded to the national Manningham Trust Student Poetry competition, sponsored annually by the National Federation of State Poetry Societies. Oregon student poets have traditionally shone on the national stage, and this year was no exception: Four Manningham winners appear in this volume of Cascadia.

The Oregon Poetry Association gratefully acknowledges the generous support of the Collins Foundation. I want to personally thank the judges who volunteered their time, as well as OPA outgoing president Eleanor Berry for her wise advice and my husband Todd Ellner for his encouragement and support. Most of all, I want to thank Oregon's teachers, students, and parents for keeping all of our dreams alive for another year.

Tiel Aisha Ansari
OPA President and 2013 Student Contest Chair

THE POETS

Division I, Kindergarten—Grade 2

Honorable Mentions

Division II, Grades 3—5

Honorable Mentions

THE POETS

Division III, Grades 6—8

Honorable Mentions

Division IV, Grades 9—12

Honorable Mentions

DIVISION

I

"Poetry is the rhythmical creation of beauty in words."

Edgar Allen Poe

YOGA

We go to yoga with our neighbors
every Sunday.

I look around.
Chicken bones stretch.
Wacky hair flies up and ties in knots.
Rocket pose wobbles up and down.

My mom and dad
cannot reach the floor—
but I can.
And I quickly go up again.

The music dances
in the sunshine.

Marilee closes her eyes.
She sees walnut trees.

I close my eyes.
I see different colors—
red, orange, green and yellow
in two circles where my eyes are.
I don't know where I'm going.

A vacuum underneath us zooms.
Mmmmmmmmmmmm

The floor is a continent for fairies.
A place to dance with toadstools,
grass and a palace.
Fairy cupcakes smell like sweet candy.

Marlene Mackzum

Marlene Mackzum, Kindergarten
Hope Chinese Charter School, Portland
Teacher: Mindy Peterson

WINTER

This is the time when
small white dreams
fall out of the sky.
The time when you walk
on the white,
cold towel
of nature.
The time when dreams
come to life and the whole earth
is covered in an everlasting
time of white crystal.
When nature
turns into one long blast
of joy and happiness.
This is the true spirit
of winter.

Leo Decker

Leo Decker, Grade 2
Willow Wind CLC, Ashland
Teacher: Lacy Kleespie

WATER

Water is the wind's blanket.
It splashes along the stream,
but at the end it reaches the ocean
as fast as if it has wings.

Loren Thompson

Loren Thompson, Grade 2
Willow Wind CLC, Ashland
Teacher: Lacy Kleespie

BLUE AIRPLANES

Soaring through the air
Like winged space shuttles going faster and faster
Until they're out of sight

Raindrops fall
They never stall the creature's wings
On and on they go until they're finally low, landing like
Small airplanes

Wings beating against the wind
Blue jays are the best
Because they're well dressed
In bright blue feathers
Flying in the flock
Staying together

Cecilia Valdovinos

Cecilia Valdovinos, Grade 2
Home Schooled, Damascus
Teacher: Krista E. Valdovinos

A POEM IN THE LIGHT

A poem in the light
While my glowing eyes shine.
Blowing in the wind
With my body left behind.
I watch the birds flutter by.
A poem in the wind
While my glowing eyes shine.
Loving the world in the wind.

Macey Pine

Macey Pine, Grade 2
Creative Science School, Portland
Teacher: Christi Braun

BLUE MOON

The moon is a lantern for the sky.
The stars are the moon's children, and
the sun is the one that shines.
And the clouds are just friends.
The night sky is the mother of all living things.

Daisy Schmeling

Daisy Schmeling, Grade 2
Willow Wind CLC, Ashland
Teacher: Lacy Kleespie

PROOF OF AUTUMN

Leaves on the ground,
fallen and broken.
Leaves on trees,
changing from green
to golden yellow.
I grabbed one,
but it stuck to my hand.

Dead long grasses
lie down flat,
covered with cobweb blankets.

Green acorns fall for squirrels.
Thousands of grapes hang down—
their vines wind up
through oak tree—sweet!
Nibble, nibble, spit!!!!!

Xavier Rauch Moore

Xavier Rauch Moore, Grade 2
Create Solutions Tutoring, Ashland
Teacher: Sara-Lynne Simpson

SOUNDS OF POETRY

Moonlight splashing together to make peaceful light evaporate

The bumping sound of fog flowing through the wet trees

Calm air getting squished into noise so graceful and cute

Noise coming together to make music in the grateful wind

Rain rushing from fierce lightning forming new calm islands

Nice noise swimming through our bodies and giving help for us
and for our world

The peaceful life of the soft glowing wind

Torin Repasky

Torin Repasky, Grade 2
Mary Rieke Elementary, Portland
Teachers: Stephanie Savage/Jill Rebholz

SUN

The sun is but another star in the universe:
not the biggest nor the smallest.
Though not biggest or smallest, it is the closest.
It is a fire—
a leaping flame with hot flares striking whenever it wishes.
The sun has its good too:
It warms the hearts of all on cold frosty days,
lighting up the whole earth.
Striking off peacocks' feathers
and the wings of finches,
making them shine.
When it is night, the cat's eyes gleam in the dark like two suns.
The sun is a star—shining on misty days,
warming the hearts of all humans, animals and living creatures in
    the wide universe.

Amy Amato

Amy Amato, Grade 2
Heritage School, Salem
Teacher: Elaine Olsen

THE SHOOTING STAR

It is like a ball of fire shooting across the galaxy.
It is like a sparkling piece of glitter.
It is like a light dancing in the shadows.
It is like a crystal ball in the sky.
It is like a guy whistling on the moon.
That is what the shooting star is like.

Mazzy Garcia

Mazzy Garcia, Grade 2
Willow Wind CLC, Ashland
Teacher: Lacy Kleespie

DIVISION
II

"Poetry is the impish attempt to paint the color of the wind."

Maxwell Bodenheim

IT FEELS LIKE

When I hear the wind
it feels like a beat to my ears.
Every step I take feels like a new adventure.
Whenever I look up at the night sky
it feels like the stars are watching over me.
When I put my feet on the grass
it feels like I am a tree
and I have roots that go into the earth.

Charlotte Angermeier

Charlotte Angermeier, Grade 3
Willow Wind CLC, Ashland
Teacher: Lacy Kleespie

I AM NOT ALONE

I am not alone
I hear him behind me
His eyes burning the back of my neck
I am not alone

I am not alone
I look up
I see the sun getting captured by a big blanket of gray
But then the sun pushes the blanket away, ripping its seams for
     the sun's rebirth
I am not alone

I am not alone
I look down at the leaves that lost a war to stay on the tree
They fought a battle long and hard, blood absorbed in the soft,
     wet dirt
I am not alone

I am not alone
But I am free as the sky
Free to be me
No one to tell me not to be
Still, I feel a burning in the back of my neck
He is still watching
I am not alone

It is silent
No one around
I am alone
But I am not alone

Talia Rosenbloom

Talia Rosenbloom, Grade 5
Portland Jewish Academy, Portland
Teacher: Harriet Wingard

RIVER

To me the river is a stream of birds
flying through the sky
whistling their long sad songs.

Harper Strong

Harper Strong, Grade 3
Willow Wind CLC, Ashland
Teacher: Lacy Kleespie

BAD DREAMS

Breathing Faster
Awful night bad and scary
Death dream, killing, dying

dark afraid, can't see my way out
roaring thunder cloud
eyeballs rolling on the ground
aaaaaaaaHHHHHHHHHH!
moldy cheese in my lunch
"Sssssssshhhhhhhhhh, why are you screaming?"

Ellie Kojima

Ellie Kojima, Grade 4
Fir Grove Elementary School, Beaverton
Teacher: Laurie Calafet

BIG OR SMALL?

How big are we really?
We think of ourselves as big and important
But if the world is huge and the universe is even bigger
and there is still more to explore then...
how big are we?
We must be as small as specks of dust or even smaller
We are not big, nor will we ever be, we are small
Smaller than dust, smaller than that even
We are small and the other ones out there are big

Samuel Rothstein

Samuel Rothstein, Grade 4
Portland Jewish Academy, Portland
Teacher: Jim Juntunen

BOB

Bob is see-thru.

He tastes like air.

He sounds like a whooshing sound.

He smells like nothing.

He looks like a hologram.

He makes me feel safe.

Max Spencer

Max Spencer, Grade 4
West Park Elementary School, Hermiston
Teacher: Kathy Dopps

FRECKLES OF LIGHT

The poke of a hummingbird through a dark blanket,
A dark but not quite scary night,
I am blind to everything around me,
Does anyone else feel as I do?

No buzzing of traffic,
Just the stars and me,
And the moon watching, and I wonder,
Will I become one of them soon?

Those freckles of light,
Bright blinks everywhere,
Almost like I could touch them, and I think,
Does each star have its own story?

And is the story they told us true?
The one with the hummingbird who made those
Pictures of the beautiful and majestic animals
Captured by a tattered coat of light.

I see a dark, black night,
With little white crumbs of bread sprinkled throughout the sky,
A blanket that gives no warmth,
Alive only because of those freckles of light,
Bright blinks everywhere.

I wonder how many stars there are,
Following some sort of invisible light towards Earth
Traveling everywhere...
It's quiet, yet too loud,
I am out of my mind with nature around me,
Those specks of light,
Are they watching over me?

Olivia Jacobs

Like guardian angels,
Each and every one of those
Freckles of light,
Bright blinks, everywhere.

Olivia Jacobs, Grade 5
Portland Jewish Academy, Portland
Teacher: Harriet Wingard

FRIENDSHIP

Friendship

Is like no other experience
It is like getting a
            new puppy
or

Being on a
            roller coaster.

Sutton Guyer

Sutton Guyer, Grade 3
Willow Wind CLC, Ashland
Teacher: Lacy Kleespie

LOVE

Love is like wind whistling its way through the trees up to the wide blue sky. Swirling and whirling, jumping and twirling,

Love is free

Callan Skuratowicz

Footnote: The orientation of this poem was adjusted to accommodate the line length.

Callan Skuratowicz, Grade 3
Willow Wind CLC, Ashland
Teacher: Lacy Kleespie

SON OF THE SHADOW

The shadow of a storm approaches,
as it's sweating rain,
dried mud softens as I slip,
and scrape my shins
I want to turn back,
but I know the past, plus my reputation is not pretty,
leaves start to swirl,
nature is putting up a fight,
as the leaves become a twister,
the sky rains lightning as the faith burns and smolders
and death takes over.

Henry Seal

Henry Seal, Grade 4
Portland Jewish Academy, Portland
Teacher: Jim Juntunen

DIVISION
III

"Poetry is thoughts that breathe, and words that burn."

Thomas Gray

PERSISTENCE OF MEMORY
Poem on a painting by Salvador Dali

A barren landscape,
Nothing stirring but ants.
Tomorrow grows and today sets,
The whisper of the dove.

Bent figures and broken time.
Titter of the ants,
And the waves on the sand.
Gaping cliff face,
With no shadow.

I now know what the ants
Are waiting for.
They are waiting for the moment that will
Never come again.

Kendrick Lee

SPECIAL NOTE: Kendrick's poem won **Second Place** in the junior division of the *NFSPS Manningham Trust Student Poetry Contest.*

Kendrick Lee, Grade 6
Spencer Butte Middle School, Eugene
Teacher: Rena Dunbar

AUTUMN

Autumn
The word whispers
Down the cracked asphalt.
It hides in the crooked shadow of the trees,
But everywhere it lurks, the leaves turn bright,
Awash with scarlet and lemon,
Lovely flames that lick the wood
And melt away to those tissue paper skeletons.
I would collect them by the hundreds
If only they didn't turn to dust
Within the day, like leprechaun's gold.
The cold metal chime of autumn
Settles into flesh and mind and bones.
The tintinnabulation calls the birds to the sky.
In preparation for the winter, they flee
And the sun is cold like an empty smile
Or pulls away, aloof behind the clouds
And turns its back,
So that the last harvest
Of the tiny fig tree, alone in my backyard
Cannot offer even its half dozen fruit
And even though the final traces of summer are fading
Right outside the door,
And all I can think about is those sad
Minute green figs,
Cold and hard and bitter,
Exposed to the season's chill
Their demise decreed by
Autumn

Gabi Cohn

SPECIAL NOTE: Gabi's poem won **First Honorable Mention** in the junior division of the *NFSPS Manningham Trust Student Poetry Contest*.

Gabi Cohn, Grade 8
Portland Jewish Academy, Portland
Teacher: Harriet Wingard

Marley Lopez

Something that comes from the heart
in a secret
cavern where the blood comes pure
it's full of the ugly truths and beautiful unknowns
the things even you don't know about yourself
breathing in and out,
you fuel the light breeze in your lungs and your body is at
peace.
Winter snow weighs your bones from the inside,
the marrow a scripture of your biology
the science of a human
what thoughts do you see behind your closed eyes?
They call it poetry

A naïve soul
She gave in too easily to her own thoughts
gracefully sweeping the darkness
groping the nightmares of the hiddens in her mind
tears show she's over-thought her nature
again
They write notes and prescribe pills
to make her city
okay
they told her sadness was depression
and prescriptions for emotions ran her life
dystopia
she wrote it down
they call it poetry

Crashing crystals
a scientific construction and destruction
shining
the light twinkled like the stars at night
home was a chandelier
delicate
beautiful
that would age gracefully
and hid no secrets inside
crystal clear simplicity
They call it poetry

FOOTNOTE: No title was given for this poem.

Marley Lopez, Grade 8
Catlin Gabel School, Portland
Teacher: Holly Walsh

ART INSPIRES

Painting
I have painted on canvas and paper
And one day will paint on my bedroom wall
I dream of a sea of blues and violets
Colors that engulf the light,
And make the darkness become radiant
Drawing
I find the grains of graphite ground into my fingers
The silver dust allowing my hands to create shading
Or a smudge that has never belonged
And I become the tool
Metal
A risk will always be present
The ferocious spark that slices the material
To work with metal
Is to create something to strive for,
Be it dance, passion, or a simple moment of tranquility
Drama
A way to express hidden secrets and passions
For the art of illusions through characters,
Characters that can touch the heart of a child
Or shred the last rays of hope
Drama creates challenges that can strengthen
Or crush the protective walls of the human mind
Sculpting
The ability to morph a simple lump
Into a magnificent image in three dimensions
Be it clay or sand on a beach battered by the salty waves
My hands become devices of creation
Alive
Is how I feel when creating yet another piece of art
Art is one of the things where form does not matter,
Art shall always be a way to say the unspoken word
The mind is the true canvas
Of the vast dream that we all strive to complete

Lila Reich, Grade 8
Catlin Gabel School, Portland
Teacher: Holly Walsh

CHRISTMAS WISH

He ran in all the time
Lifted us over his shoulders
Then threw us down
Right before we got to the Christmas tree

He called us monkeys
And potatoes
Depending on if we're upside down
Or hanging over those big clubs he calls shoulders

Now he just lies in his bed
With his hand over his heart
Like he's afraid it will burst out
I watch him do this day by day

These past five years
We make our Christmas wishes
The wish I want to come true the most
Is for my grandpa to be cured
From this game of old

Logan Rothell

Logan Rothell, Grade 7
Eagle Point Middle School, Eagle Point
Teacher: Rick Taylor

I AM A BRANCH

I am a branch of my teacher
She teaches me to be brave
She teaches me not to be scared of things
That come from my imagination,
But...
To conquer those fears you
Grow
a little higher.

I am a branch of my teacher
She teaches me I am individual
She teaches me I am who I am and
    Nobody
Can
Chop
Me
Down.

Leila Kenner

Leila Kenner, Grade 6
Willow Wind CLC, Ashland
Teacher: Lacy Kleespie

NEVER AGAIN

A Teardrop, Walking down the cheek of its owner
A Feather, Skydiving from its bird
Both sadness;
Both lost, forever

A Drop of blood, jumping off its owner
A drop becomes a stream
Soon, all the blood has fallen

A knife, wrapping itself in a velvet blanket
A Camera, Looking at the sight,
The images burned in its mind, for it shall never forget what it just
witnessed

The last words, slowly walking out of his mouth
a dead body, falling down like a ragdoll

A coffin, hugging the body inside of it
A funeral, a life, walking away from us all
It will never come, or so it seems, until it does

Nathan Bray

Nathan Bray, Grade 7
Eagle Point Middle School, Eagle Point
Teacher: Heather Hohnstein

ROSE WINDOW SCRIPTED

Iridescent stories—
people captured in glass
led by fluttering
birds.

Shining bright—
red, blue and green
ripples wave,
forming flowers.

Colorescent animals
swirl by—
soldered into delicate
dazzle.

Superb puzzle precision—
primary shapes cut
small and
joined.

Orange, pink and purple bump
through celestial sheets of glass,
where light reveals
spectacular mysteries.

Amaya Acosta-Lieb

SPECIAL NOTE: Amaya's poem won **Fourth Place** in the junior division of the *NFSPS Manningham Trust Student Poetry Contest.*

Amaya Acosta-Lieb, Grade 7
Create Solutions Tutoring, Ashland
Teacher: Sara-Lynne Simpson

SOMETHING HAPPENS

In your hands

You hold this poem

Wondering why you're reading this

You sink into the words

And become the poem itself

While you're dreaming in your world

Something happens

Something happens

While you're dreaming in your world

And become the poem itself

You sink into the words

Wondering why you're reading this

You hold this poem

In your hands

Korynn Fitzjarrell

Korynn Fitzjarrell, Grade 6
Creswell Middle School, Creswell
Teacher: Kim Kuhnhausen

WHERE I'M FROM

I am from the mountains
From the rolling hills
From the rushing streams
The fields of lupine and vetch
The tall old growth forests
The warm sunny rock to eat your lunch on.

I am from the valley
From the large wide meadows full of brown and green grass,
From the cool powerful sound of Bear Creek,
The thin paper birch trees peeling in the wind.
I'm from the warm summer sunshine.

I am from the desert.
From the wonderful powerful smell of sage,
The cold nose-biting wind,
The tall high bleak mountains of snow surrounding my campsite,
From the warm hot spring wrapping me in a steamy mist.
I'm from watching the sun rise and the moon set.

I am from the ocean,
From the sound of the rolling, crashing waves lulling me to sleep,
The feel of the gritty sand under my feet.
I'm from the smell of the salty spray.

I am from all the homes I've ever lived in,
A cozy little apartment above a garage where I was born,
A large airy house in the mountains
And a small apartment in town.
I'm from the view of the hills out my back window,
From "you should wash your hair tonight,"
From my cat Lion and my guinea pigs.
I'm from home.

Lela Miatke

I am from music,
From the sound of fiddle, guitar and piano playing all together,
From playing my violin,
I am from the sound of blended voices singing in harmony.

I am from my past, present and future,
All woven together into one big strand that will never break.

SPECIAL NOTE: Lela's poem won **Second Honorable Mention** in the junior division of the NFSPS Manningham Trust Student Poetry Contest.

Lela Miatke, Grade 6
Willow Wind CLC, Ashland
Teacher: Lacy Kleespie

DIVISION
IV

"Poetry lifts the veil from the hidden beauty of the world,
and makes familiar objects be as if they were not familiar."

Percy Bysshe Shelley

COMPASS ROSE

When you want something, close your mouth;
when you want someone,
open your eyes.
Do not wait for the night-hours to come to you
and whisper where to go from here.
There are compasses
on your palms even if you are afraid
to read them.
Grab the world until it coughs
and taste the dust motes that fall
from Heaven
onto the floor of your bedroom.
Everything you waste your shooting stars
on is only sitting in the shadows
waiting for you to cry out yes.
Yes.
Pay attention to the stories the world tattoos
onto your tongue
while you are too busy writing and erasing
your own.
Decide what you would give up heaven for. Chase it
until your lungs bleed sunsets
and dirt roads beat their whispers
onto the bare souls of your feet.
Run away, but run in circles
and hold your map tight in your teeth. Wait
until the paper dissolves
and the roads blur
and in that moment you know a new way to
find home.

Julia Renner

Julia Renner, Grade 12
St. Mary's Academy, Portland
Teacher: Sara Salvi

Madison Cho-Richmond

BATTLES

They are the children who call three a.m. their home.

The cashier-laundromat operator-mother of three
who works to live another day but finds herself
in the same place every sunrise.

Those nursing home incarcerates who refuse to stop
counting out candles for their birthday cakes.

The man who now lives in a soggy cardboard box
because he stepped out of his closet.

Older siblings who choose
to tuck their brothers and sisters into bed.

Fighters with machine guns and grenades
and razor blades and concave stomachs.

Sneaker-kicking court-siders and the ones who are too afraid to try.

Dreamers, make-believers, carpe diems of any kind.

And anyone else who counts each balloon of her lungs.

Madison Cho-Richmond, Grade 10
Lake Oswego High School, Lake Oswego
Teacher: Lisa Mitchell

SATISFACTION

It is in the last sentence of a paper you feel it.

The first tooth you lost
its slimy shine tied to a long piece of floss
dripped red as you presented it to your mother like a clean room or a 4.0.

The eve of your 14th birthday stung your tongue and fingertips with it
you're too old for things
but still so young.

It's the home before midnight
the first kiss outside of your white knobbed door
he lingered a little too long by your mouth,
his nose kissed you before his lips did,
but you still felt it as he walked back to his car
you could still smell him on your
skin.

You're sitting in an audience
listening to a song sung by a girl whose thoughts are made of clouds
and your body is not your body anymore
so much so that when you lift your arm to dry soaking cheeks
you feel sorry for whoever's tears they are,
but they're yours
and they're beautiful.
She's singing the blues and she's your sister and you never want
to let go of this moment

Like when you turned 14
or when he kissed you on your doorstep
or when you presented your tooth with arms stretched like innocence
or in that last sentence of a paper

And you felt it.

Kiah Bacon, Grade 12
St. Mary's Academy, Portland
Teacher: Sara Salvi

DIVORCE

Their wedding rings,
the ones that had been thrown
into the fire burned
red as the woods outside.
Chaos surged like barbed rain
maddening foxes,
rash silver blazes
through the creek bed.
Fear beckons
as an ember filled coffin
forcing owls' eyes to swell
in wakefulness.
Gentle fauna
peels from trees,
laying cerise foot prints
among paths
attempting to walk
the smoldering land.
Their skin peels, ripping
like glue from paper.
The skeleton
of a vacant home
stood
burning.
Destroyed.

Samantha Spliethof (sidebar)

Samantha Spliethof, Grade 12
Eagle Point High School, Eagle Point
Teacher: Jay Schroder

END OF THE WORLD

Sunday...
And it's raining.
The fire died down,
The smell of burnt flesh lingers.
I like the rain.
It purifies the air that scorches lungs
With every breath of that unholy sacrament
We humans left are forced to partake in.
Fragrant rose petals fall from the sky.

Stuart Springs

Stuart Springs, Grade 12
Eagle Point High School, Eagle Point
Teacher: Jay Schroder

KNOWLEDGE

Why don't animals speak our language?

Are their tongues too heavy and slow?
Too thick for spoken word
Slurring every letter
Into simpler sound?

Or maybe it's the brain inside the hard bone skull.
As dull as the fluid around it
Unaware and clueless
That human word exists?

Or could it be they're hiding something?
Hidden secrets unknown
Taunting us
Locked under silent tongues

We have to know.
We make clean cuts through flesh and fur
Digging in with scalpels and needles
And when dead flesh yields few results
We move on to slaughter the next.

Jaimie Green

Jaimie Green, Grade 12
Eagle Point High School, Eagle Point
Teacher: Jay Schroder

MALE POETS DO SOMETHING TO MY INSIDES

Their words find a way to sink beneath my skin.
Their voice crouches low in their throat,
Too deep to be reached,
Too damp to be comfortable,
Too warm to be left,
Each syllable warm and wet behind my ear,
Each stanza a hand tucked into my spine.
A challenge waits in the tip of their nails
And the bite of their tongue.
They deliver lines as blows,
They deafen your ears with harsh retellings.
They peel back their confidence,
To show their insecurities.
Male poets stand with one hand in their pocket
And one hand reaching out to feel the next sound,
They pick apart your words,
Looking for something they can use,
To mold into their poetry,
To expose you to their audience.
A smirk resides in the corner of their lips.
The tug of their words
Pulls the air from my lungs.
Male poets do something to my insides.

Miranda Pruett

Miranda Pruett, Grade 12
Eagle Point High School, Eagle Point
Teacher: Jay Schroder

MISMATCHED EXPECTATIONS

Father and son expectations and alma maters
What about the mismatch?
Who thinks of fathers and daughters?

Everyday same routine, leaving early off to work
She listens in her pink bedroom the door unlatched
Father and son expectations and alma maters

Your med school diploma neat and tidy on the wall
She touches it gently, fingers stretching
Who thinks of fathers and daughters?

She dreams of being a dancer, twirling in an empty studio
Or a musician with a cello, finding a melody that fetches
Father and son expectations and alma maters

You want her to become a politician making speeches
To do something to brag about, something better than making sketches
Who thinks of fathers and daughters?

Like a pink sock in a black shoe or a crème brûlée with water
They never really go together, but can't be pulled apart
Father and son expectations and alma maters
Who thinks of fathers and daughters?

Fiona Ferguson

Fiona Ferguson, Grade 11
Cleveland High School, Portland
Teacher: Alex Gordin

PRODIGY'S PARLOR

An open mind is full of flippancy and inconsistency.
Tides break away from their constricting schedules
They are bound to on Earth.
They roll in and out as they please,
Through open ears and eyes and hearts and souls.
Rushing past, flittering behind eyelashes,
Pulling the beholder one way,
And then another,
In a beautiful, endless conniption of intoxicating dizziness.
But along that torrent of life lie little eddies,
Where tired thoughts take time to rest.
And sigh.
And banter languidly.
And if one looks here, into this prodigy's parlor,
At teatime on a hot Summer's day,
A slow snapshot of such an open mind can be sketched,
But only by equally flippant fingers.

Anisha Datta

Anisha Datta, Grade 11
Glencoe High School, Hillsboro
Teacher: Bill Huntzinger

THE DUSTIEST CORNER OF MY MIXED-UP SOUL

I am the murky puddles on the side of the road
The ominous gray storm clouds overhead
And a sudden chill up unzipped jackets.

I am the weed among flowers
The unforgiving thorn on an innocent rose
And stubborn, barren soil.

I am the suspicious red smudge on a page of a library book
A candy wrapper blowing along the sidewalk
And the fingerprints on a dirty restroom mirror.

My mind is dangerous and uncharted
Filled with potholes and quicksand
And beasts unforeseen by a leery traveler.

My disposition is a chain to the blistered feet
Of tired refugees begging for rest
Who've walked miles in worn-out shoes.

So come in and take a load off
In the dustiest corner of my mixed-up soul
And I'll show you what cannot be unseen.

When you leave, take a piece of my crumbling heart
For the long trip home, like all the others have:
It will stick to your aching ribs for a lifetime.

Abigail Leyes

Abigail Leyes, Grade 9
Bend Senior High School, Bend
Teacher: Matt Viles

Photography by Judy Hayden
Eugene, Oregon

"To be a poet is a condition, not a profession."

Robert Frost

OPA History:

Founded in 1956, the Oregon Poetry Association (OPA) is Oregon's oldest literary organization, and with over 350 members, we are Oregon's largest literary organization. OPA was a statewide outgrowth of Portland's Verseweavers Poetry Society, which was founded in 1936. The OPA constitution and by-laws were created in April of 1956, and the first annual meeting was held in April of 1957.

David Hedges, who was OPA President from 1982-1983 and 1997-2002, revitalized the organization during his second term. He initiated the Student Poetry Contest, Poetry Day readings at book stores, and the Family Poetry Workshop Project. He was instrumental in the society's success.

OPA Members:

We welcome all poets, regardless of publishing history, academic background, or writing experience. Our membership includes winners of the Oregon Book Award (Ingrid Wendt, Willa Schneberg, Penelope Schott and Judith Montgomery), Pushcart Prize nominees, Academy of American Poets award winners, journal editors, and small press editors, as well as beginning poets, poets with a recent first chapbook publication, and experienced poets with no publication history. Our past board members include former Oregon Poet Laureate William Stafford, and the current Oregon Poet Laureate, Paulann Petersen, is an OPA member. Our members reflect the variety of poetry writing in Oregon.

OPA's Mission:

The mission of the Oregon Poetry Association is to:
— build and sustain a diverse community of Oregon poets
— provide Oregon poets opportunities to exchange ideas and learn from one another
— further the appreciation of poetry throughout the state
— raise awareness of Oregon poets.

www.oregonpoets.org

Collins Foundation Grant:

The 2013 OPA Student Poetry Contest was supported by a generous grant from the Collins Foundation. OPA gratefully acknowledges its support.

2013 Manningham Award Winners:

All winners' poems in Divisions III and IV were entered in the National Manningham Trust Poetry Contest sponsored by the National Federation of State Poetry Societies (www.nfsps.com). Ten prizes are awarded in each division: First Place—$75, Second Place—$50, Third Place—$40, Fourth Place—$35, Fifth Place—$30, and five Honorable Mentions—$10 each. All winning poems will be published in the Manningham Trust Poetry Student Award Anthology. Winners will receive complimentary copies. The schools of each winning student will receive a complimentary copy for the school library. The top winning poems will be read to NFSPS members at the Convention held in June 2013.

Congratulations to our four Oregon 2013 Manningham Award winners in the Division III Category:

— **Second Place**: *Persistence of Memory*, Kendrick Lee, Spencer Butte Middle School, Eugene, Oregon. Teacher: Rena Dunbar.

— **Fourth Place**: *Rose Window Scripted*, Amaya Acosta-Lieb, Create Solutions Tutoring, Ashland, Oregon. Teacher: Sara-Lynne Simpson.

— **First Honorable Mention**: *Autumn*, Gabi Cohn, Portland Jewish Academy, Portland, Oregon. Teacher: Harriet Wingard.

— **Second Honorable Mention**: *Where I'm From*, Lela Miatke, Willow Wind CLC, Ashland, Oregon. Teacher: Lacy Kleespie.

www.ingramcontent.com/pod-product-compliance
Lightning Source LLC
Chambersburg PA
CBHW060618030426
42337CB00018B/3105